all about my mother

Like mother, like daughter.

AUTHOR UNKNOWN

all about my
mother

Cheryl Saban PhD

*While we try to teach our children about life, our
children teach us what life is all about.*

AUTHOR UNKNOWN

RYLAND
PETERS
& SMALL
LONDON NEW YORK

Senior Designer Sonya Nathoo
Commissioning Editor Annabel Morgan
Picture Research Emily Westlake
Head of Production Patricia Harrington
Art Director Leslie Harrington
Publishing Director Alison Starling

First published in 2011 by
Ryland Peters & Small
20–21 Jockey's Fields
London WC1R 4BW
and
519 Broadway, Fifth Floor
New York, NY 10012
www.rylandpeters.com

ISBN 978-1-84975-087-5
Printed and bound in China.

contents

introduction

The bond that emerges between mums and daughters can
be profoundly nurturing and fulfilling, while at the same time
complicated and confusing. Women are generally social creatures,
and the relationships we form with other females are among our
most treasured. We often nurture such relationships over a
lifetime. But the mother-daughter relationship is the queen of
them all. It is the classroom for every little girl's stockpile of
behaviors, and the breeding ground for the positive as well as
not-so-positive traits and tricks she'll use to navigate through life.

The way we think about, feel for, and treat our daughters has
a lifelong impact on how they live their lives, and very much
affects how they interact with us. The ability to enhance the

mother-daughter bond and to enjoy a good relationship with one another requires open communication, acceptance, honesty, mutual respect, attention, validation and unconditional love. Finding a harmonious way to balance the need to be close to our mothers and/or daughters, and yet to distance ourselves and differentiate from them as well, can be difficult, and, for some, takes years. But the journey is transformative. We have so much of value to share.

What follows is a collection of mother-daughter stories gathered from around the globe. As you read, I hope you'll ponder your own experiences as a mother, daughter, grandmother, and reflect on the wisdom you've gained from your own unique journey.

Chance made you my daughter,
love made you my friend.

AUTHOR UNKNOWN

bonding

in the beginning

Mothers have been staring into the eyes of their newborns since life began, and babies have gazed right back. Both are imprinting knowledge of each other deep inside the brain, where it will endure. While this relationship is a primal part of the cycle of life, it feels a little less mysterious when we gaze into the faces of daughters. Why? Because we know the challenges she'll face…after all, we're girls too.

Ironically, this foresight in no way ensures that the journey mothers and daughters embark upon will be an easy one. In fact, the mother-daughter relationship can be described as a roller-coaster ride of extreme ups and downs. The hopes and dreams that mothers have for their daughters are all bound up with preconceptions of what they should or should not do – based primarily on what we experienced when we were young girls ourselves. We want to save our daughters from the mistakes we made, but we don't always know how to express this or, more importantly, to teach it. Sometimes we just make it up as we go along.

It's never too late to expose our children to unconditional love and understanding. As they say, 'What goes around comes around.' The best we can strive for is to give our daughters memories worth repeating.

"The minute my first child was born, I was flooded with a new sensation, a yearning to protect and hold close. It was as if a strong, territorial force compelled me to stay nearby – and I was shocked by the emergence of a love so profound that I could scarcely describe it. Though everything about having a baby and being a mother was new to me, I recognized my part intuitively, and felt a primal bond. I took her to my breast, my eyes fixed on her small face, and I became an instant authority on all things concerning her."

"Mother-daughter bonding means something very specific to me. When I hear this phrase, I don't think so much about how close we are, though this is surely a factor. I ponder the time when I learned what my daughter has become. She is amazing. And I am grateful, because I know that in some small way, I am a part of that."

Nothing is worth more than this day.

JOHANN WOLFGANG VON GOETHE

Love without conditions, and encourage your daughter's dreams.

"When I was six years old, our family was on summer holiday. One of our favourite activities was miniature golf. We were on the last hole, and it was my turn. I swung the club, and accidentally hit my mother in the face and broke her nose. I was horrified, yet my mother clapped, and made a big fuss about how exciting it was. I had hit a hole-in-one, and it was a very big deal for a six-year-old. Mum never complained about her broken nose. She was proud of me! I still feel guilty about that golf game and mum's broken nose, even though she passed away ten years ago. A mother's love is a remarkable thing."

"Bonding with her daughters was a day-to-day affair for my mom. She loved to cook and always made sure we all ate together. She had us girls prepare the table and do the dishes. She taught us to do most of the household chores on our own. She was a disciplinarian, but a loving one. We witnessed her generosity, as well as her determination never to let anyone oppress our family or deprive us of our rights. She managed on her own to send us to school. I learned everything from my mom — especially how to be strong. She kept our family together."

"I enjoy a wonderful relationship with my daughters. Our bond is based on our desire to provide each other with an emotionally safe place that we can always depend on, no matter what happens in our individual lives."

All our knowledge has its origins in our perceptions.

LEONARDO DA VINCI

Seek harmony and peace.
Love truly, forgive quickly.

"My mother is my rock. She taught me how to face adversity, rise above it and come out stronger. A single mother, she moved across the country to give us a fresh start. She has always been a symbol of love and strength for me. If it wasn't for her wisdom and guidance, I wouldn't be the woman I am today. Every day, I wake up wishing I could give her the life she always dreamed of. The one thing I can always give her is my love."

"My five year old loves listening to me tell stories about myself when I was her age. I enjoy telling them too, and find them to be extremely bonding because they help me remember how I felt, and how I saw the world at that young and innocent age. These stories put into perspective the things I expect from her, and she enjoys the feeling that we are in fact much closer than the 25 years between us."

"As a toddler, my daughter became enthralled with the scent of my perfume, the aroma of the fabric softener I used in our laundry and, well, just the regular smell of me. Whenever we went out into public places, she'd bury her face in my skirt, and breathe deeply. I didn't realize it at the time, but my daughter was insecure and frightened, and my smell made her feel secure and safe when she wasn't feeling much of either. I had recently remarried, and traveled regularly for my job, which meant that she and her sister often had to stay behind with a babysitter. I found out later in life that my daughter's experiences with babysitters weren't always pleasant ones. Her quirky habit of smelling me – burying her head in my clothes to breathe in my fragrance – came from her need to keep me close. Breathing me in was her way of expressing her fear of abandonment, and her need to feel safe and protected. To this day, every time we hug, my daughter and I take deep, long breaths, and feel comforted and connected by the familiar smell of each other."

*Good actions give strength to ourselves,
and inspire good actions in others.*

PLATO

Learn to adapt;
be aware that change
is inevitable.

"When I was little, my mom did all sorts of crafty things. She sewed most of my clothes, my dance costumes, and all my fancy Easter dresses. Though she never claimed to be a great cook, nobody could make Chili con Carne like my mom. She seemed chronically busy, her work never done, yet she managed plenty of affection for me when I needed it, and never complained when I followed her around and bothered her. Looking back, I took it all for granted. I recognize now that although we had our arguments, she always managed to love me unconditionally. She showed by example that love was at the top and bottom of everything. Somehow she knew I'd figure things out in time. She was right. Thanks, Mom."

"My mum is my best friend. She's the one support system that has never failed. She is there for me no matter what, at any time. She is my hero."

"As a grown woman, having truly grounded and centered myself within who I am in this world, I feel I am finally able to give back to my mom on a deeper level than I recognized was possible when I was younger. We are sisters, friends, mother and daughter and soulmates."

"When my eight-year-old was still in my womb, I remember being overwhelmed by waves of unconditional love for this angelic being that was going to share blissful mother-daughter moments with me. Now, instead of being partners on the same team, we are sometimes bitter rivals in an exhausting handball game of who's right. But at night, glancing at her serene sleeping face, I have romantic hopes that she and I will do wonderful things together when she moves beyond this stage. Actually, I think my own mother is still waiting for this!"

A son is a son till he takes him a wife, a daughter is a daughter all of her life.

IRISH SAYING

sharing and growing

recognizing the need to be different

As mothers, we set the first boundaries, but we also open the first doors. There is a push-pull dynamic at work that can be confusing for all involved. First and foremost, we want to safeguard and protect our daughters, while at the same time we recognize that we must allow them the freedom they need to meet their own challenges.

As our daughters grow from tiny babies to women who walk out the door to begin independent lives of their own, we must navigate constant changes. These changes are essentially life lessons comprised of experiences that run the gamut from ecstasy to agony. Mothers ask themselves questions: did we make too many mistakes? Were we too kind or too tough? Did our daughters learn the right lessons? Did we allow them to have enough fun? Are they mentally and physically healthy? Did we love them enough? Did we make them feel secure, respected, accepted, included?

Basically, we worry, and we do that with regularity, regardless of how young or old our daughters are. Worry and concern are a big part of a mother's job, and I think most of us would agree that we do this part exceptionally well!

The heart that truly loves never forgets

PROVERB

"When I was four or five, my mother took me by train to see the National Ballet perform *Giselle*. I remember it as if it were yesterday… sitting on the train, going to the theater, watching the ballet with my mouth open, thinking there could never be anything more beautiful. My mom had a great sense of culture, which she passed down to me."

"I lost my mother when I was 21. Today, even as an adult woman, I still think of her first when faced with a problem or when I need advice. I don't remember her doing or saying anything extraordinary to create our bond; she just always did whatever was in the best interest of her daughter. She kept it simple. Her words matched her actions. I felt safe and connected. Throughout my life, without any conscious thought, I selected other women to help me through rough times; situations that would ordinarily prompt a phone call to one's mother. I think I was so grounded in the bond I shared with my mother that I instinctively knew to whom she would want me to turn. Our bond lived on after her death and gave me the power to help myself. What a gift."

"As a daughter you have the fortune to be cared for by your mother; the question is, do you have the intelligence to appreciate her? We each love, fight, learn and grow from each other. I had the luck to appreciate my mother before she passed away – before her time – and the luck of having two amazing daughters of my own (plus two sons). I am one of the lucky ones. Tell your mother *now* how much you appreciate her, and tell your daughters how much they are worth!"

"My mom is my best friend and confidante. Since I was young, she has had so many responsibilities, yet I've never felt like anything less than her number one priority. When I reflect on this statement, it is beyond me, considering I was the oldest of six children and she had a very overbearing husband – essentially her seventh child. I could always go to my mother for anything and everything and she has never made me feel judged, or that there was a problem with no solution."

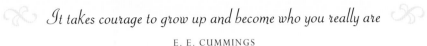

It takes courage to grow up and become who you really are

E. E. CUMMINGS

"Sadly, my mother-daughter bond wasn't created with happy memories. My recollections of my developing years are filled with disappointments and betrayal. But because of my own unpleasant experiences, or perhaps despite them, I found my own strength. I was determined to become a different kind of mother, and I am. I learned to forgive, even though it meant keeping my distance from a dysfunctional situation. Ultimately I have learned to be a caring, compassionate and loving mother to my own child, and this is a legacy I am proud to share."

Help each other
heal - forgiveness
works wonders.

Tell me and I'll forget. Show me and I may not remember. Involve me and I'll understand.

INDIAN PROVERB

"As a child, my mum allowed me to search, discover and find my way with support, love and understanding. She taught me to be open-minded and compassionate. Mum has been my voice of reason and my confidante through the years. I value her love and our friendship more than I can express and I am acutely aware that having a mother who is also one of my best girlfriends is one of the greatest gifts a daughter can be given."

"I learned so much from my mother: how to cook, how to become a lady. But mostly I learned that we are all here to help one another. My mother would do anything to help someone in need. She taught me that it was important to make the world a better place – that, in effect, we are our brothers' keepers. I treasure this as one of the most important lessons she taught me."

"At one particularly rocky stage of our mother-daughter relationship, one of my daughters and I didn't speak for three months. She was in her late teens. We had gotten into a row about something that seems insignificant now, but had seemed quite important then. It was a boundary issue – she had not complied with some rule or other, and I had been unwilling to allow her to be who she was. Whatever the cause of the rift, it was one of the hardest times of my life. I can't remember what finally brought us both back together, but it was a miracle, and our mutual joy was ecstasy. I learned a huge lesson from that experience – we both did. Nothing – *nothing* – is worth losing your relationship with your child. Communication and mutual respect is key. We are all individuals. Our children are not possessions that can be kept, and we, as parents are not things that can be discarded. I am so grateful that we rediscovered our sanity, and our love. She is a treasure – a unique and beautiful soul – and I am so very grateful for her in my life."

Respect each other.
Let go of limiting beliefs
and attitudes

You can't always get what you want.
Find your middle ground.

"My relationship with my mom soured when I went to college. I rebelled and tried to prove my independence by resisting what she tried to teach me. After my career got going and I was on my own, I discovered that I liked a lot of things that my mother loves, such as working in the yard and cooking. During these awakenings I've learned that a lot of what she taught me was true. Even though our bond has been a half circle at times, we have come to have a good relationship and I love my mother. The more we mature, the more I appreciate her and ask questions, because I know there will come a day when no answers will be available, only history."

"I once confided in my grown daughter, that I feared I'd made mistakes as a young mother, and hoped she didn't feel as though she'd gotten a bad deal in the 'mom' department. She turned to me with a beautifully tender smile and said, 'Mom, you're absolutely perfect. You always did the best you could – I know that. I love you bigger than the sky. Don't worry.' It made my heart sing. I must have done something right to have a daughter who could respond so compassionately."

*And ever has it been
known that love knows
not its own depth until
the time of separation*

KAHLIL GIBRAN

reconnecting,
and learning to let go
making peace and sharing wisdom

Mothers and daughters are constantly redefining their roles. As mothers, we continually reconfigure our places in our daughter's lives. We learn to roll with the changes, to become mentors rather than managers, to eventually let go without, of course, actually letting go…it's magic. And as daughters, we learn how to maintain a connection with our heritage – to be gracious and grateful to our mothers, to bring the best of their lessons to bear in our own lives with our own daughters, even if we do in fact choose to chart a different course with our own little girls. So be it.

At the end of the day, love triumphs over all. *I love you*. Three little words. Don't be stingy with them. Cherish the moments that made you smile. Your mom was probably doing the best she knew how, with the tools she was given. One thing is sure: the mother-daughter bond transcends both time and place. Although it may wax or wane at various ages and through life's many stages, it is nevertheless something tangible, for most of us, throughout our lives. It's important to record, share and treasure these memories, for they are ours to keep when our moms are gone.

"My mother-in-law had two sons. In her culture, this was the highest of joys. But in some ways, her good fortune was also bittersweet. She shared with me her regret that she didn't have a daughter with whom to share womanly things. But in time, she opened her heart to me, daughter-in-law that I was, and we formed a bond of our own which has had its own sweetness. Her wisdom has been a blessing."

"Mom was famous for her apricot pie. She served it for her dinner parties and never went to a social event without one. Even though my role was limited to sous-chef, I never felt as close to my mom as when I was standing next to her at the stove while she stirred the pot of fresh apricots and told me stories from her childhood. Like her mother before her, my mom knew instinctively how much sugar and butter to add. My favorite job was rolling out the piecrust. If we were short on flour, we would turn the pie into a crisp with oatmeal and brown sugar topping. On the very rare occasion when mom used a store-bought piecrust, that crust became our secret."

Learn to appreciate the wisdom gained by a lifetime of experiences.

"My daughter's husband's mum passed away suddenly – a tragedy for the entire family. She was too young, too vibrant, and we were all shocked. I watched my daughter comfort her husband through the loss of his precious mother, and soothe their young children through the bewilderment of their grandmother's death. My daughter's ability to console everyone around her was awe-inspiring. Where did she come by this strength? When we hugged over the course of those days, and our eyes met, no words were necessary. We are both so aware of our mother-daughter bond, and how special and fleeting it is. We no longer take it for granted."

Celebrate your differences,
and encourage exploration

"One of my favorite moments in life was waking up to my grandma singing loudly downstairs. I rubbed my sleepy eyes but her joyful bursts of song were so appealing that I had to investigate! As I crept down the stairs, she saw my sister and me and ran over singing, 'it's raining, it's raining!' in a very high and glorious opera-sounding song. I looked outside and indeed it was a cloudy, rainy day, but my grandma turned a gloomy day into one of the most magical moments of my life. To this day when I wake up to rain my heart leaps with excitement. I love rainy mornings. Thanks grandma. What a treasure you gave me – one of many!"

51

"My daughter and I bond on many levels, but often the roles have been reversed. I have 20 more years of life experience than her and believe myself to be an old soul, but there have been many times when my daughter seems even older. She came to me with an inner knowledge that only an experienced soul could possess. Even as a youngster, she helped me with the evolution of my own spirituality and, ultimately, the evolution of my true self."

"My brother, who has spina bifida, suffered a massive seizure one morning, and my mom and I worked together to get him to the hospital. Mom was an ER nurse at the time, and the panic and fury in the emergency room was so intense that the doctors and nurses tending to him, including my mom, didn't realize I was at my brother's head the whole time, holding onto him, talking him through it. Thank God they were able to revive him. Seeing my mom in action, forced to be a nurse and a mom at the same time, gave me a whole new appreciation for not only her profession, but for her as our mom as well."

Anger and intolerance are the enemies
of correct understanding.

MOHANDAS GANDHI.

"The relationship I have with my mum is one of love, and a knowing that she's always there for me if I need her. I don't live at home and we're both busy with our own lives, so we don't get the opportunity to meet up and do 'girlie' things very often. However, we never let a day go by without texting each other, asking how the day went, and telling one another how much we love each other."

"Each year my relationship with my daughters grows deeper, more precious and more unique. I adopted all three of my girls (and threw them into a household as a single, working mom with two biological sons). What we have all realized over the years is that being someone's biological child is not what makes you someone's daughter or son, and being someone's biological parent is not what makes you a good mother. If you pay attention to each of the unique individuals whom you call your children, they will over time, through trial and error, and after countless successes and mistakes, teach you everything that you need to know in order to be a great parent."

"I was lucky to have my maternal grandmother living close to us during my childhood. The bond we had was amazing. It was like having two moms – one for the practical everyday life and one for the fantasy life – a perfect blend. We became four generations when I gave birth to my two daughters. It was great for us to have so many women in our household. I had my Oma in my life until I was 47 years old. What a blessing."

"I lost my mother suddenly when I was six months pregnant with my first son, her first grandson. My first thought when I was told the news was '*my baby!*' I didn't really know why those two words shouted out in my mind as I collapsed into my sister's arms. Three months later, when my first beautiful boy was born, I understood absolute and unconditional love. This baby is now twenty-two. Over the years I have so poignantly missed my mother's input and, much as I've tried to be as patient as her, I know I have not succeeded. Now I know absolutely that those two words rung out so clearly in a primal scream because of what we would all miss. Our mother."

A loving heart is the truest wisdom.

CHARLES DICKENS

"Our hearts need love, in particular a mother's love. My mother was my best friend and my inspiration. She perished on Flight 11, 9/11, but her love will last forever. Her love has left an eternal imprint on my soul."

"My youngest daughter – the youngest of four children, three of them girls – was once quiet and shy. She had a hard time connecting to others when she was little but, aside from some turbulent teenage years, always connected well with me. From her earliest grade-school days, she took great pains to create unique gifts for me on special occasions. These gifts were handmade, and always included photographs of the two of us together. She intuitively understood and celebrated the mother-daughter bond from the very beginning. Now, as I watch her mature into a grown-up woman who is no longer so shy, but is still as creative and compassionate, I treasure those gifts more than words can express."

And finally...

Mothers are fonder than fathers of their children because they are more certain they are their own.

ARISTOTLE

All About My Mother is a tribute to mothers and daughters everywhere. Though the history of your own mother-daughter relationship may be compiled of both happy memories and disappointments and complications, the lessons we learn from our mothers, our daughters and, if we're lucky, our grandmothers too, helps to define how we behave with others, and how we treat ourselves as well.

Coming to terms with this most important, complex relationship is a worthy goal. Having the willingness to reflect upon and share the lessons we've learned along the way will help us reconnect with the joy that is possible within this primal female bond. And whether we feel that our moms did their job well, or that they missed the mark to some degree, one thing is certain: we can all seek to be fully and open-heartedly grateful for the first and most important treasure our moms gave us: the gift of life.

So, celebrate the gifts your mother gave you, and make peace with any challenges she might have presented too. Accept that no one ever promised life would be easy and, sometimes, the magic just doesn't work. When that is the case, take the lessons you've learned and the hard knocks you've endured, and find the silver lining. With a little effort and reflection, you can achieve a sense of harmony, gratitude, and peace that will enhance your quality of life. And then you can pass that on. Namaste.

Picture Credits

ph = photographer

Pages 1 & 2 ph Debi Treloar; 4 ph Debi Treloar/the family home of Nicky Sanderson, co-owner of Lavender Room in Brighton, East Sussex (www.lavender-room. o.uk); 5-7 ph Polly Wreford; 8 & 9 ph Debi Treloar; 10-11 ph Polly Wreford; 13 ph Debi Treloar; 14 ph Debi Treloar/the home of Debbie Johnson, owner of Powder Blue (www.powder-blue.co.uk); 15 ph Sandra Lane/Ros Fairman; 17 ph Debi Treloar; 18 ph Debi Treloar/the home of Rosie Harrison, co-owner of www.aandrphotographic.co.uk and www. airspaces.co.uk; 19 ph Caroline Arber; 20 ph Debi Treloar; 21 ph Claire Richardson; 22 ph Polly Wreford/a family home in west London by Webb Architects and Cave Interiors www. caveinteriors.com & www.webb-architects. co.uk; 24 ph Sandra Lane; 25 ph Claire Richardson; 26 ph Polly Wreford/the family home of Alison Smith in Brighton; 27 ph Polly Wreford; 28-29 ph Claire Richardson; 30 ph Paul Massey/the home in Denmark of Charlotte Lynggaard, designer of Ole Lynggaard Copenhagen (www.olelynggaard.dk); 33 ph Debi Treloar; 34 background ph Caroline Arber; 34 inset ph Sandra Lane; 35 ph Debi Treloar/Debbie Johnson as above; 36 ph Debi Treloar/Ros Fairman; 38 ph Polly Wreford; 39 ph Debi Treloar/the home of Jenny Atherton, co-owner of Lavender Room in Brighton (as above); 40 ph Sandra Lane; 42 ph Debi Treloar/www.juliaclancey.com; 43-45 ph Claire Richardson; 46 ph Polly Wreford; 47 ph Debi Treloar/Bed of Flowers, B&B owned by Floriene Bosch www.bedofflowers.nl; 48 ph Debi Treloar; 49 ph Winfried Heinze; 50 ph Debi Treloar; 51 background ph David Montgomery; 51 inset ph Jan Baldwin; 52 ph Polly Wreford; 53 & 54 ph Debi Treloar; 57 ph Debi Treloar/Jenny Atherton as above; 58 ph Sandra Lane; 60-61 ph Polly Wreford; 63 ph Polly Wreford/Atlanta Bartlett www.paleandinteresting.com.

*A mother's happiness is like a
beacon, lighting up the future but
reflected also on the past in the
guise of fond memories.*

HONORÉ DE BALZAC

Acknowledgments

Thank you for spending a moment with me and with all the incredible women who shared their stories for this book. Though I haven't revealed the names of specific individuals, rest assured that these experiences come from the real women who lived them.

I feel enormously blessed to have given birth to three daughters and one precious son. We surround each other with love and affection and are tied together with an invisible cord that will connect us throughout time and space – the memories we share will form a legacy they'll pass on to their own children.

I lovingly and wholeheartedly dedicate this book to my own mother, Betty Aileen. I treasure the bond I have with her. At this stage of my life, I can appreciate it for what it is – precious and unbreakable, perfect in its own way. I respect her, adore her, and honor her for all she accepted, labored, tolerated, and bore – with love, smiles, hugs, even tears – endlessly without end, throughout her life – for me.

I love you, Momma. Thank you for everything.